C000017287

ICAEW
Management Information

First edition 2007, Thirteenth edition 2019

ISBN 9781 5097 8175 1

British Library Cataloguing-in-Publication Data
A catalogue record for this book is available from the British Library

Published by

BPP Learning Media Ltd,
BPP House, Aldine Place,
142–144 Uxbridge Road,
London W12 8AA

www.bpp.com/learningmedia

Printed in the United Kingdom

Welcome to BPP Learning Media's **Passcards** for ICAEW **Management Information**.

- They **save you time**. Important topics are summarised for you.

- They incorporate **diagrams** to kick start your memory.

- They follow the overall **structure** of the ICAEW Study Manual, but BPP Learning Media's ICAEW **Passcards** are not just a condensed book. Each card has been separately designed for clear presentation. Topics are self contained and can be grasped visually.

- ICAEW **Passcards** are **just the right size** for pockets, briefcases and bags.

- ICAEW **Passcards focus on the exams** you will be facing.

Run through the **Passcards** as often as you can during your final revision period. The day before the exam, try to go through the **Passcards** again! You will then be well on your way to passing your exams.

Good luck!

Contents

Preface

1: The fundamentals of costing

The classification of costs is an essential management accounting technique. The aim of the cost accounting system is to provide information to do the following:

- Calculate the cost of a product or service
- Compare actual costs to budgeted costs
- Work out prices for contracts

Make sure you are familiar with the terms used here for the different types of cost. These appear later in the syllabus when we look at unit costs.

Topic List

What is cost accounting?

Basic cost concepts

Cost classification – inventory

Cost classification – planning

Cost classification – control

Ethics

Cost accounting provides information to

- Establish inventory valuations (Chapter 2)
- Plan (Chapter 6)
- Control (Chapter 9)
- Make decisions (Chapter 5)

(Note that IAS 1 changes the titles of financial statements as they will be used in IFRSs.

1 'Balance sheet' will become 'statement of financial position'

2 'Income statement' will become 'statement of profit or loss'

3 'Cash flow statement' will become 'statement of cash flows'

Entities are not required to use the new titles in their financial statements. Consequently these passcards may use these terms interchangeably.)

Managing involves

- Planning
- Controlling
- Decision making

The management accountant

provides the manager with

- assistance in planning
- assistance in controlling
- assistance in decision making

The data used to prepare financial accounts and management accounts are the same. The differences between these accounts arise because the data is analysed differently.

Financial accounts

- Prepared for external individuals
- Detail performance of a defined period
- Legal requirements for limited companies to prepare FA
- Format of published FA determined by
  - Law
  - SSAPs
  - FRSs
  - IASs
- FA cover business as a whole
- FA information monetary (mostly)
- Historic picture of past operations

Management accounts

- Prepared for internal managers of an organisation
- Aid management in recording, planning and controlling organisation's activities
- Help decision-making process
- No legal requirements to prepare MA
- Format of MA at discretion of management
- MA can focus on specific areas of an organisation's activities
- MA incorporate non-monetary measures
- Historic record and future planning tool

Cost unit

is the basic measure of a product or service for which costs are determined.

Example

- Patient episode (in a hospital)
- Barrel (in the brewing industry)
- Room (in a hotel)

Cost object

is anything for which we are trying to ascertain the cost.

Example

- The cost of a product
- The cost of a service
- The cost of operating a department

Composite cost unit

is a cost made up of two parts, for example patient/day cost.

Direct cost

is a cost that can be **traced in full** to the cost unit.

Direct costs include

- Direct materials
- Direct labour
- Direct expenses
- Total direct costs = prime cost

Indirect cost (overhead)

is a cost that is incurred whilst making a product but which **cannot be traced directly** to the cost unit.

Indirect costs include

- Indirect materials
- Indirect labour
- Indirect expenses } = production overhead
- Administration overhead
- Selling and distribution overhead

Total product cost

Product cost → identified with product

Period cost → deducted as expense

| What is cost accounting? | Basic cost concepts | Cost classification – inventory | **Cost classification – planning** | Cost classification – control | Ethics |

Fixed cost

is a cost which is unaffected by changes in the level of activity within a relevant range.

Graph of fixed cost

Cost £

Fixed cost

Volume of output (level of activity)

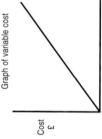

Example

- Rent of a building
- Business rates
- Salary of a director

Variable cost

is a cost which tends to vary with the level of activity. The variable cost per unit is the same for **each unit** produced.

Graph of variable cost

Cost £

Volume of output (level of activity)

Example

- Direct materials
- Direct labour
- Sales commission (varies with volume of sales)

Semi-variable/semi-fixed/mixed cost

are costs that are part-fixed and part-variable and are therefore partly affected by changes in the level of activity.

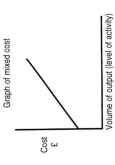

Graph of mixed cost

Cost £

Volume of output (level of activity)

Example

- Telephone bills
- Sales person's salary

Relevant range and stepped costs

are fixed in nature but only within certain levels of activity.

Cost £

Volume of output (level of activity)

Example

- Supervisors' salary costs
- Royalties

Responsibility accounting

segregates revenues and costs into areas of personal responsibility to monitor and assess performance of each part of an organisation.

Responsibility centre

is a department or organisational function whose performance is the direct responsibility of a specific manager.

Controllable costs

can be influenced by management decisions and actions.

Uncontrollable costs

cannot be affected by management within a given time span.

Fundamental principles

Integrity	Members must be straightforward and professional in all business relationships.
Objectivity	Members should avoid all bias, prejudice and partiality.
Professional competence and due care	Members must not perform roles which they cannot without reasonable care, competence and diligence. They must stay technically up to date and comply with professional standards.
Confidentiality	Members should not disclose confidential information without permission or legal or professional right or duty.
Professional behaviour	Members should protect their reputation and that of the professional body.

2: Calculating unit costs (Part 1)

The management information system provides information on unit costs as the basis for management planning and control.

Inventory valuation is used to value materials for management accounts and for financial reporting purposes.

Topic List

Direct and indirect costs

Inventory valuation

| | Direct and indirect costs | | Inventory valuation |

Direct material cost

is all material becoming part of the cost unit. It forms part of the **prime cost**.

Direct labour costs

are all wages paid for labour. They form part of the **prime cost**.

Direct expenses

any other costs (other than direct material cost and direct wages) incurred on a specific cost unit. They are part of the **prime cost**.

Indirect cost (overhead)

is a cost that is incurred whilst making a product but which **cannot be traced directly** to the product, service or department.

We'll use the following information about receipts and issues of materials in the remainder of this chapter.

Date	Receipts		Issues		Balance	
	Quantity	Value	Quantity	Value	Quantity	Value
	Units	£	Units	£	Units	£
March 1					10	100
March 10	30	450				
March 12			25			
March 20	20	320				
March 23			15			

FIFO

FIFO assumes that materials are issued out of inventory in the order in which they were delivered into inventory.

Example - FIFO

	£
March 12 issue = $(10 \times £10) + (15 \times £15)$ =	325
March 23 issue = $15 \times £15$	225
Closing inventory = $20 \times £16$	320
	870

Advantages ☑ and disadvantages ☒

- ☑ Logical, represents what is physically happening
- ☑ Easy to understand and explain
- ☒ Inventory valuation based on replacement cost
- ☒ Cumbersome to operate
- ☒ Cost comparison and decision making difficult due to price variations
- ☒ Issue prices can lag behind market value if inflation is high

FIFO is an historical cost method.

Advantages ☑ and disadvantages ☒

☑ Issues are at close to market value

☑ Current costs used in decisions

☒ Cumbersome to operate

☒ Opposite to what is physically happening

☒ Difficult to explain

☒ Decision making can be difficult due to price variations

LIFO

LIFO assumes that materials are issued out of inventory in the reverse order to which they were delivered.

Example - LIFO

	£
March 12 issue = 25 × £15	375
March 23 issue = 15 × £16	240
Closing inventory = (5 × £16) + (5 × £15) + (10 × £10)	255
	870

Material issues are based on market value.

Cumulative weighted average

involves calculating a weighted average price by dividing total cost by total number of units in inventory. A new average price is calculated when a new receipt of material occurs.

Example

	£
March 12 issue at £(100 + 450)/40	343.75
= £13.75 × 25	
March 23 issue at £((13.75 × 15) + 320)/35	225.60
= £15.04 × 15	
Closing inventory = 20 × £15.04	300.80
	870.15

(The 15p is a rounding difference)

Advantages ☑ and disadvantages ☒

- ☑ Price fluctuations are smoothed out so decision making is easier
- ☑ Easier to administer than FIFO and LIFO
- ☒ Resulting price rarely an actual price
- ☒ Prices lag a little behind market values if there is gradual inflation

Periodic weighted average pricing

is an average method where a single average is calculated at the end of the period based on all purchases for the period.

Periodic weighted average price $= \dfrac{\text{Cost of opening inventory} + \text{Total cost of receipts in period}}{\text{Units in opening inventory} + \text{Total units received in period}}$

Unless stated to the contrary, assume the cumulative average method (rather than the periodic average method) is required in an exam question.

FIFO, LIFO and cumulative weighted average inventory valuation methods produce different costs of sales and hence profits

Opening inventory values and purchase costs are the same for each method

Therefore different costs of sales are due to different closing inventory valuations

Profit differences = differences in closing inventory valuations

3: Calculating unit costs (Part 2)

Management need to know the full cost of items for certain decisions. These decisions include determining selling prices and valuing finished goods inventory.

There are two main methods for sharing indirect costs between cost units. These are absorption costing and activity based costing.

*These methods treat fixed production overheads as **product costs** which are then added to the cost of inventory.*

Topic List

Absorption costing (AC)

Activity based costing (ABC)

Costing methods

Other approaches

Allocation

Allocation is the process by which whole cost items are charged directly to a cost unit or cost centre.

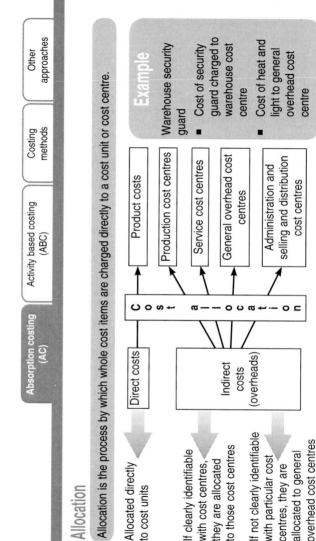

Direct costs

Allocated directly to cost units

Indirect costs (overheads)

If clearly identifiable with cost centres, they are allocated to those cost centres

If not clearly identifiable with particular cost centres, they are allocated to general overhead cost centres

Cost allocation

- Product costs
- Production cost centres
- Service cost centres
- General overhead cost centres
- Administration and selling and distribution cost centres

Example

Warehouse security guard

- Cost of security guard charged to warehouse cost centre
- Cost of heat and light to general overhead cost centre

Apportionment

The first stage of overhead apportionment is the identification of all overheads as production, service, administration or selling and distribution.

Overheads within general overhead cost centres

- Share out between other cost centres
- Use a fair basis of apportionment

The second stage of overhead apportionment is to apportion the costs of service cost centres (both directly allocated and apportioned) to production cost centres. This is known as reapportionment.

Method

- Apportion costs for service cost centre with largest costs first
- Then other service cost centres are apportioned between production cost centres

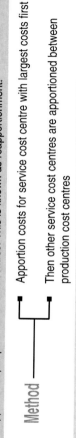

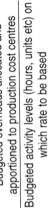

| Absorption costing (AC) | Activity based costing (ABC) | Costing methods | Other approaches |

The final stage in absorption costing is the absorption of overheads into product costs using overhead absorption rates (OARs).

Predetermined OARs

Many overheads are not known until the end of a period. Waiting until the end of the period would cause delays in invoicing, inventory valuations and so on. Random fluctuations in overheads would create variable OARs from month to month.

Budgeted overheads allocated and apportioned to production cost centres

Budgeted activity levels (hours, units etc) on which rate to be based

Bases of absorption

- Per unit (identical units)
- Per direct labour hour (labour intensive)
- Per machine hour (machine intensive)

Departmental OARs

- Used instead of blanket (single factory) OARs
- Reflect different times spent by different products in production cost centres

Over-/under-absorbed overheads

These arise because the OAR is predetermined from budget estimates. When actual overheads incurred and overheads absorbed using predetermined OARs differ, there will be an over or under absorption of overheads.

Reasons
1 Actual OH ≠ budgeted OH
2 Actual activity level ≠ budgeted activity level
3 1 and 2 above (together)

Accounting for over/under absorption of overheads

INCOME STATEMENT

Under-absorbed overhead

DR (expense)

INSUFFICIENT absorbed overhead

Over-absorbed overhead

CR (expense reduction)

TOO MUCH absorbed overhead

Inadequacies of absorption costing

- **Unit costs are distorted by absorption rates** of, say, 300% of unit labour costs and so cost information is misleading

- **Overheads are hidden** within **unit production costs** and so are not controlled

- It tends to **allocate too great a proportion of overheads** to **high-volume products** (which cause relatively little diversity) and too small a proportion to low-volume products (which cause greater diversity and use more support services)

Modern manufacturing environment

- Costs tend to be **fixed** and **overheads** are a much greater proportion of total costs.
  - Manufacturing is capital and machine intensive
  - AMT

- There has been an **increase in support services** (such as production scheduling).
  - These services assist in the manufacture of a wide range of products.
  - They are **unaffected by changes** in production volume.
  - They **vary** instead with the **range** and **complexity** of products

Outline of an ABC system

1. Identify an organisation's **major activities**.

2. Identify **cost drivers**.

3. Collect the costs associated with each activity into **cost pools**.

4. Charge **support overheads** to **products** on the basis of their **usage** of the **activity** (measured by the number of the activity's cost driver they generate).

Cost drivers

are any factor which causes a change in the cost of an activity.

Examples

The cost driver for a cost that varies with production volume in the short term (such as power costs) should be volume related (eg, labour hours or machine hours).

The cost driver for a cost that is related to the transactions undertaken by the support department where the cost is incurred should be the transaction in the support department (such as the number of production runs for the cost of setting up production runs).

Example

Cost of goods inwards department totalled £10,000. **Cost driver** for goods inwards activity is **number of deliveries.** During 20X0 there were 1,000 deliveries. 200 of these deliveries related to product X. 2,000 units of product X were produced.

Cost per unit of cost driver = £10,000/1,000 = £10

Cost of activity attributable to product X = £10 × 200 = £2,000

Cost of activity per unit of product X = £2,000/2,000 = £1

Types of overhead activity

Overheads associated with ...	such as ...	are driven by ...
Unit related activities	Cost of lubricating oil	Units produced/hours worked
Batch related activities	Two models of car on one production line	A number of products being made with the same facilities
Product sustaining activities	Type approval of vehicles	The number of different products
Facility sustaining activities	Factory insurance	The organisation being in business

Features of job costing

- Work is undertaken to customers' special requirements
- Each order is of short duration
- Jobs move through operations as a continuously identifiable unit
- Jobs are usually individual and separate records should be maintained

└─ Job costs are collected on a job cost sheet/card

A job

is a cost unit which consists of a single order or contract.

Profit on jobs

Profit may be expressed either as a percentage of **job cost** (such as 15%) (25/100) mark-up or as a percentage of **price**, such as 20% (25/125) margin.

Batch costing

is very similar to job costing.

$$\text{Cost per unit} = \frac{\text{Total batch cost}}{\text{No. units in batch}}$$

Contract costing

is a method of **job costing** where the work undertaken is bespoke and costs involved are significant. A formal contract is made between the customer and supplier.

Features of contract costing

- **Formal contract** between supplier and customer
- Work is undertaken to **customer's special requirements**
- Work is for a **relatively long duration**
- Work is frequently **constructional** in nature
- The **costing method** is similar to **job costing**
- The work is frequently **based on site**

Overhead costs

are added **periodically** based on predetermined OAR.

Contract accounts

are job or WIP accounts recording the direct costs and overheads charged to the contract.

Process costing

is used where it is not possible to identify separate units of production so costs are averaged. Typical process costing uses are in oil refining, food and drink and soap manufacture.

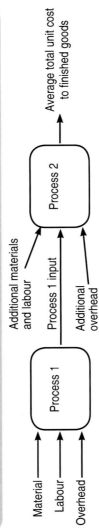

Process costing can also be applied in a service environment. For example, in an organisation that provides a shirt laundering service the processes involved might be as follows:

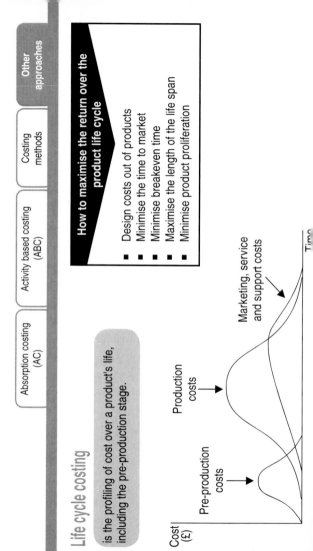

Absorption costing (AC) | Activity based costing (ABC) | Costing methods | Other approaches

How to maximise the return over the product life cycle

- Design costs out of products
- Minimise the time to market
- Minimise breakeven time
- Maximise the length of the life span
- Minimise product proliferation

Life cycle costing

is the profiling of cost over a product's life, including the pre-production stage.

Cost (£)

Pre-production costs

Production costs

Marketing, service and support costs

Time

Traditional approach to product costing

1 Develop a product

2 Determine the expected standard production cost

3 Set a selling price (probably based on cost)

4 Resulting profit

Costs are controlled through variance analysis at monthly intervals.

VS

Target costing approach

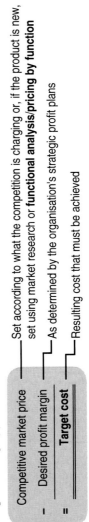

	Competitive market price	Set according to what the competition is charging or, if the product is new, set using market research or **functional analysis/pricing by function**
−	Desired profit margin	As determined by the organisation's strategic profit plans
=	**Target cost**	Resulting cost that must be achieved

Absorption costing (AC)	Activity based costing (ABC)	Costing methods	Other approaches

JIT systems

Traditional responses to the problems of improving manufacturing capacity and reducing unit costs of production

- Longer production runs
- Economic batch quantities
- Fewer products in the product range
- More overtime
- Reduced time on preventative maintenance, to keep production flowing

Just-in-time systems challenge such 'traditional' views.

Although often described as a technique, JIT is more of a philosophy since it encompasses a commitment to continuous improvement and a search for excellence in the design and operation of the production management system.

JIT consists of JIT purchasing and JIT production.

JIT purchasing

Materials are delivered just-in-time.

JIT production

Production is driven by customer demand.

Elimination of waste, involvement of all staff and continuous improvement are the three key elements of the JIT philosophy.

Operational requirements

- High quality
- Speed
- Reliability
- Flexibility

- Efficient production planning
- Reliable sales forecasting

JIT and cost management

Cost reduction in:

- Warehousing
- Capacity utilisation is improved
- Waste
- Write-offs reduced

Notes

4: Marginal costing and absorption costing

Marginal costing treats all fixed costs as **period costs** so that these are excluded from the costs used in valuing inventory. This approach means that marginal costing and absorption costing produce different inventory valuations. Therefore profit figures will also be different under the two systems.

Topic List

Marginal costing (MC)

MC and AC compared

Contribution

equals (sales revenue – variable (marginal) cost of sales). It is short for contribution towards covering fixed overheads and making a profit.

Marginal cost

is the cost of one unit of product/service which would be avoided if that unit were not produced/provided = variable cost.

Marginal costing

- Only variable costs charged as cost of sales
- Closing inventories are valued at marginal cost
- Fixed costs are treated as period costs
- Period costs are charged in full to the income statement
- If sales increase by one item, profit will increase by contribution for one item
- Contribution per unit is constant at all levels of output and sales

The difference in reported profits is calculated as the difference between the fixed production overhead included in the opening and closing inventory valuations using absorption costing.

MARGINAL COSTING → Closing inventories are valued at marginal production cost

ABSORPTION COSTING → Closing inventories are valued at full production cost

Inventory levels

Increase in a period
- Absorption costing reports higher profit
- Fixed overheads included in closing inventory
- Cost of sales decreased
- Hence, profit higher

Decrease in a period
- Absorption costing reports lower profit
- Fixed overheads included in opening inventory
- Cost of sales increased
- Hence, profit lower

RECONCILIATION

£

Marginal costing profit X
Adjust for fixed overheads in inventory:
+ increase / – decrease X/(X)
Absorption costing profit X

Marginal costing (MC)

Arguments in favour of absorption costing

- ☑ Fixed production costs are incurred in order to make output and so it is only 'fair' to charge all output with a share of these costs
- ☑ Closing inventory will be valued in accordance with accounting standards
- ☑ Appraising products in terms of contribution gives no indication of whether fixed costs are being covered

Arguments in favour of marginal costing

- ☑ It is simple to operate
- ☑ There are no arbitrary fixed cost apportionments
- ☑ Fixed costs in a period will be the same regardless of the level of output and so it makes sense to charge them in full as a cost of the period
- ☑ It is realistic to value closing inventory items at the (directly attributable) cost to produce an extra unit
- ☑ It focuses on variable costs which are most likely to change as a result of a decision

5: Pricing calculations

The calculation of a selling price for goods or services is an important management decision.

Ideally, a selling price will cover costs and still encourage customers to buy.

Organisations often transfer goods and services internally. Transfer prices cover these transfers and give signals to management to encourage optimal decision-making.

Topic List

Full cost-plus pricing

Marginal cost-plus pricing

Mark-ups and margins

Transfer pricing

In practice, cost is one of the most important influences on price.

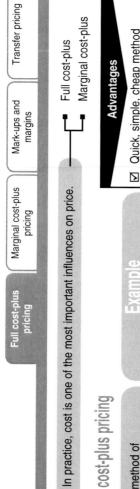

— Full cost-plus
— Marginal cost-plus

Full cost-plus pricing

is a method of determining the sales price by calculating the full cost of the product and adding a percentage **mark-up** for profit.

Example

Variable cost of production (product A) = £4 per unit

Fixed cost of production (product A) = £3 per unit

Price is to be 40% higher than full cost

Full cost per unit = £(4 + 3) = £7

$$\text{Price} = £7 \times \frac{140\%}{100}$$

$$= £9.80$$

Advantages

☑ Quick, simple, cheap method

☑ Ensures company covers fixed costs

Disadvantages

☒ Doesn't recognise profit-maximising combination of price and demand

☒ Budgeted output needs to be established

☒ Suitable basis for overhead absorption needed

Marginal cost-plus pricing

is a method of determining the sales price by adding a profit margin onto either marginal cost of production or marginal cost of sales.

Advantages

- ☑ Simple and easy method
- ☑ Mark-up percentage can be varied
- ☑ Draws management attention to contribution

Disadvantages

- ☒ Does not ensure that attention paid to demand conditions, competitors' prices and profit maximisation
- ☒ Ignores fixed overheads – so must make sure price high enough to make profit

Example

Direct materials (product B) = £15
Direct labour (product B) = £3
Variable overhead (product B) = £7
Price of product B = £40

Profit = £40 – £(15 + 3 + 7) = £15

$\text{Profit margin} = \dfrac{£15}{£25} \times 100\% = 60\%$

Full cost-plus pricing

Sales price = full cost of the product + % mark-up for profit

Marginal cost-plus pricing/mark-up pricing

Sales price = marginal cost of production (or marginal cost of sales) + % mark-up for profit

Margins and mark-ups

With a cost/profit/sales structure of:

	%
Cost	80
Profit	20
Sales	100

Profit may be expressed as:

- A % of **cost of sales** eg, 25% (20/80) **mark-up**
- A % of **sales** eg, 20% (20/100) **margin**

Examples

If the full cost of product X is £200 and a 25% **return on sales** is required, selling price = £200/0.75 = £266.67.

Investment in product Z is £1,000,000 pa and a return of 20% is required. If a unit of Z costs £100 and 20,000 units will be sold, the selling price based on this **target return on investment** is:

$$\frac{\text{expected revenue (= required return + expected cost)}}{\text{units}}$$

$$= ((£1,000,000 \times 20\%) + (£100 \times 20,000)) / 20,000 = £110$$

If product K sells for £60 and the mark-up is 20%, the cost of K = £60/1.2 = £50

If Product B costs £100, a selling price based on a margin of 25% = £100/0.75 = £133.33

Transfer prices based on market price

Where a perfect external market exists and unit variable costs and selling prices are constant, the ideal transfer price (ie, the opportunity cost of transfer) will be one of the following.

- External market price
- External market price less savings in selling costs

How to set transfer prices

1 Recognise the levels of output, external sales and internal transfers that are best for the company as a whole.

2 Arrive at a transfer price that ensures all divisions maximise their profits at this same level of output (ie, there should not be a more profitable opportunity for individual divisions).

Aims of transfer pricing

- Promote divisional autonomy
- Equitable divisional performance measurement
- Overall corporate profit maximisation

Transfer prices based on opportunity costs

Transfer price per unit = standard variable cost in the transferring division + opportunity cost to the organisation as a whole for supplying the unit internally.

Transfer prices based on cost

If there is **no external market**, the transfer price has to be based on cost.

1 **Standard or actual?** The use of standard costs is fairer because if actual costs are used the transferring division has no incentive to control its costs – it can pass on its inefficiencies to the receiving division.

2 **Variable cost?** The transferring division does not cover its fixed costs (although this problem can be overcome by central decisions or by some form of **dual pricing** or **two-part charging** system).

3 **Full cost?** The transferring division makes no profit.

4 **Full cost plus?** What margin will all parties perceive as fair?

Goal congruent decisions will be made if the transfer price is set in the range where:
variable cost in the transferring division < net marginal revenue in the receiving division

6: Budgeting

*A budget is a **plan for the forthcoming period**.*

It shows the detail of authorised expenditure that may be incurred on each type of cost during the period.

The budget therefore acts as a plan and an authorisation for managers to incur costs in the period.

Budgets are also used to control spending or monitor variances.

Topic List

Budget uses and framework

Steps in preparation

Master budget

Traditional budget problems

Preparing forecasts

Alternative approaches

The responsibility for preparing budgets should lie with the managers who are responsible for implementing them.

- Sales manager → sales budget
- Purchasing manager → material purchases budget
- Production manager → direct production cost budgets

Reward for managers can be built into the budget process and their achievement of budget targets.

Uses of budgets

- Planning
- Communication
- Coordination
- Responsibility accounting
- Control
- Motivation

Budget committee functions

- Coordinating and allocating responsibility
- Issuing the budget manual
- Timetabling
- Providing information
- Comparing actual and budgeted results

Budget manual contents

- Explanation of budgetary process objectives
- Organisational structures
- Outline of principal budgets
- Administrative details of budget preparation
- Procedural matters

The order of budget preparation

1 Identify the principal budget factor ────── The factor which limits the activities of an organisation

2 Prepare a sales budget (units of product **and** sales value) and then a finished goods inventory budget (to determine the planned change in finished goods inventory levels)

3 Prepare a production budget (sales ± budgeted change in finished goods inventory levels, in units)

4 Prepare production resources budgets (materials usage, machine usage, labour)

5 Prepare a materials inventory budget (to determine the planned change in materials inventory levels)

6 Prepare a raw materials purchases budget in units and value (usage ± budgeted change in materials inventory)

7 Prepare overhead budgets

8 Prepare the **master budget (budgeted income statement, budgeted balance sheet, cash budget)**

Master budget

is a consolidation of all the subsidiary budgets.

= Budgeted income statement

+ Budgeted balance sheet

+ Cash budget

Sensitivity analysis

shows the effect of changes in budget assumptions on the budget.

Examples

If sales revenue falls by 10%, how is profit affected?

Problems with traditional budgets

- Expensive
- Time consuming
- Quickly out-of-date
- Inflexible
- Based on inaccurate forecasts

A **forecast** is an estimate of what might happen in the future

Linear relationships

A linear relationship can be expressed as $y = a + bx$.

If there is a linear relationship between total cost and level of activity then

y = total costs a = fixed cost

x = level of activity b = unit variable cost

Cost forecasting with the high-low method

1. Select the periods with the highest and lowest activity levels.

2. Deduct the cost of the low activity level from the cost of the high activity level, and calculate the variable cost per unit (difference in variable costs ÷ difference in activity levels).

3. Calculate fixed cost (total cost at either output level – variable cost for output level chosen).

Linear regression analysis

is a statistical technique for establishing a straight line equation to represent a set of data.

Correlation

is the extent to which the value of a dependent variable is related to the value of the independent variable.

Perfect positive correlation

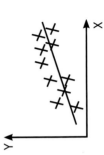

Partial correlation

Degrees of correlation

- Perfectly correlated
- Partly correlated
- Uncorrelated
- Non-linear or curvilinear correlation

Values of r

- r = +1 = perfect positive
- r = −1 = perfect negative

No correlation

Non-linear or curvilinear correlation

Coefficient of determination, r^2

r^2 measures the proportion of the total variation in the value of one variable that can be explained by variations in the value of the other variable.

$$\text{If } r = 0.9, \; r^2 = 0.81$$

If the correlation coefficient of two variables = 0.9, we know the variables are **positively correlated**. The coefficient of determination, $r^2 = 0.81$ and this gives a more meaningful analysis. We know that 81% of the variations in the value of y **could** be explained by variations in the value of x.

Note: we do not conclude that 81% of variations in y are caused by variations in x. We say that 81% of variations in y can be explained by variations in x.

Forecasts can be improved with the use of big data.

Big data

It concerns 'high-volume, high-velocity and high-variety information assets that demand cost-effective, innovative forms of information processes for enhanced insight and decision making.' (Gartner)

Data analytics

The process of collecting, organising and analysing large sets of data to discover patterns and other information which an organisation can use for its future business decisions.

Big data benefits

- Predicting customer demand
- Identifying customer preferences

Big data problems

- Traditional forecasting tools cannot cope
- Raises questions about benefits vs infringement of rights
- Security
- Possibility of incorrect data

Machine learning

is where computers learn to do things using examples (ie lots of data) rather than following pre-programmed rules. Forecasting can be done using machine learning and the forecasts get better as more data is analysed.

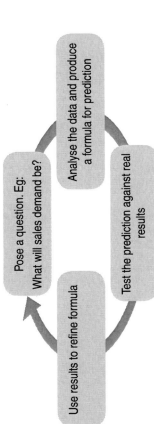

Pose a question. Eg:
What will sales demand be?

Analyse the data and produce a formula for prediction

Test the prediction against real results

Use results to refine formula

Better forecasting leads to better management decision making.

Two budget-setting styles

- Imposed (from the top down)
- Participative (from the bottom up)

Participative approach

Advantages

☑ More realistic budgets

☑ Co-ordination, morale and motivation improved

☑ Increased management commitment to objectives

Disadvantages

☒ More time-consuming

☒ Budgetary slack may be introduced

☒ Does not suit some employees

Imposed style

Advantages

- ☑ Include strategic plans
- ☑ Enhance co-ordination
- ☑ Reduce time taken to draw up budget
- ☑ Include senior management view

Disadvantages

- ☒ Low morale
- ☒ Acceptance of goals could be limited
- ☒ Stifle lower level initiative
- ☒ Team spirit may disappear

Incremental budgeting

involves adding a certain percentage to last year's budget to allow for growth/ inflation.

contrast with

ZBB

treats the preparation of the budget for each period as an independent planning exercise: the initial budget is zero and every item of expenditure has to be justified in its entirety to be included.

Advantages and disadvantages

Incremental

- ☑ Easy to prepare
- ☒ No incentive to try and reduce costs
- ☒ Budgetary slack and wasteful spending

ZBB

- ☑ (Hopefully) removes budgetary slack
- ☑ Identifies and removes inefficient and/or obsolete operations
- ☑ Forces employees to avoid wasteful expenditure
- ☒ Involves time and effort

Rolling budgets

Instead of preparing an annual budget for the full budget period, this process involves the preparation of budgets every one, two, three or four months. Each budget covers the next 12 months so that the current budget is extended by an extra period as the current period ends.

If a rolling budget is prepared every three months, the first three months of the period would be planned in great detail and the remaining nine months in less detail because of increased uncertainty about the longer-term future.

Why set rolling budgets?

- Effect of a suspected new competitor cannot be quantified when the budget is set
- Inflation is very high or is expected to rise/fall

Rolling budgets

Advantages

☑ They reduce uncertainty.

☑ An up-to-date budget is always available.

☑ Realistic budgets are better motivators.

☑ Planning/control is based on a recent plan.

Disadvantages

☒ They involve more time, effort and money.

☒ Frequent budgeting can have a detrimental effect on managers.

It might actually be simpler to update the annual budget once or twice during the year.

Alternative budget structures

Product based budgets

are **separate budgets for each product.** These are aggregated for senior management who can still look at individual product budgets.

Activity based budgets

are based on a **framework of activities. Cost drivers are** used to prepare budgets.

Responsibility based budgets

segregate budgeted costs and revenues into areas of personal responsibility. Budgetary control is based on budget centres with budget holders.

Beyond budgeting

is an approach that suggests that budgets should be more adaptive and that this can be achieved by adopting 12 beyond budgeting principles:

Leadership principles

- Purpose
- Values
- Transparency
- Organisation
- Autonomy
- Customers

Management processes

- Rhythm
- Targets
- Plans and forecasts
- Resource allocation
- Performance evaluation
- Rewards

https://bbrt.org/the-beyond-budgeting-principles/

7: Working capital

The management of working capital components – inventory, payables, receivables, cash – is a very important part of managing a business's finances. Treasury management relates specifically to the management of the business's cash.

Topic List

Working capital management

Cash operating cycle

Managing inventory

Managing payables and receivables

Treasury management

Cash budgets

Working capital = Receivables + Inventory + Cash − Payables

Managing working capital

Hold cash to pay debts ⟶ Liquidity vs Profitability ⟶ Invest cash to generate profit

Holding cash reduces risk of insolvency ⟶ Risk vs Return ⟶ Invest cash to generate profit

Remember that profit and cash flows are not the same. It is crucial for a business to maintain a sound liquidity position.

Working capital decisions

- Manipulate ratios to see effect of decision on risk/return

- Calculate revised cash operating cycles to see effect on liquidity

- Look at ratios/cycles used by similar companies

Solving liquidity problems

- Reduce inventory-holding period
- Reduce production period
- Reduce credit period for customers
- Improve cash collection
- Extend credit period from supplies (pay later)

Working capital = current assets − current liabilities

Cash operating cycle

Cash operating cycle is the length of time between cash being spent at start of production and cash being received from customer.

= Average time raw materials are in stock

less: Period of credit taken from suppliers

plus: Time taken to produce goods

plus: Time taken by customers to pay for goods

- Retailers often receive cash, pay for supplies by credit
- Wholesalers mainly buy and sell on credit, need short-term borrowings
- Small companies may have trouble obtaining credit, but may have to offer generous credit terms

Useful ratios

Current ratio

$$= \frac{\text{Current assets}}{\text{Current liabilities}}$$

Quick (liquidity) ratio

$$= \frac{\text{Current assets excluding inventory}}{\text{Current liabilities}}$$

Average payables payment period

$$= \frac{\text{Average trades payables}}{\text{Annual purchases}} \times 365$$

Average receivables collection period

$$= \frac{\text{Average receivables}}{\text{Annual sales revenue}} \times 365$$

Averages should be used where available but year end figures should be used if not.

7: Working capital

Inventory

- Raw materials and components
- Spare parts/consumables
- Work-in-progress
- Finished goods
- Goods purchased for resale

Uses up cash but generates returns

Liquidity vs Profitability

Reasons for holding inventory

- Buffer to meet demand
- Avoid risk of stockouts
- Avoid reliance on supplier lead times
- Ensure continuity of production
- Take advantage of quantity discounts and special promotions

- Buy at low price ahead of rises
- Order infrequently $\Rightarrow$ reduced ordering costs
- Seasonality of demand
- Suppliers insist on minimum order quantities

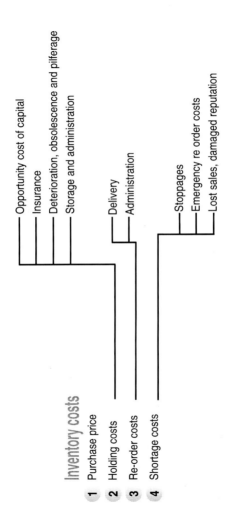

Inventory costs

1. Purchase price

2. Holding costs
   - Opportunity cost of capital
   - Insurance
   - Deterioration, obsolescence and pilferage
   - Storage and administration

3. Re-order costs
   - Delivery
   - Administration

4. Shortage costs
   - Stoppages
   - Emergency re order costs
   - Lost sales, damaged reputation

Inventory control systems

- **Re-order level system** – the optimum quantity is ordered once inventory level reaches a certain level eg, two-bin system

- **Periodic review system** – levels are reviewed at certain points in time, and a variable amount is reordered at each point

- **ABC system** – A – high value/importance, closely monitored

  B – lower value/importance, less frequently monitored

  C – least important, not closely monitored

- **Economic order quantity (EOQ)** – calculates how much to order and when, taking into account:

  c – cost of placing one order

  d – estimated usage over a particular period $EOQ = \sqrt{\dfrac{2cd}{h}}$

  h – cost of holding one unit for that period

- **Just-in-time system** – deliveries flow straight through to production/resale, so minimum inventory is held. Requires flexibility, quality, close relations with with suppliers and rationalised layouts

- **Perpetual inventory** – inventory movement in and out monitored on computer, with re-orders triggered automatically (expert system)

Managing trade payables

Advantages of trade credit

- Convenient and informal
- Low cost
- Available to most businesses
- Settlement discount may be available
- Provides subsidy for new products
- Flexible in short-term

Costs of taking too long to pay

- Damaged credit status
- Raised prices to compensate suppliers
- Loss of discount for early payment

Improving payables management

- Weigh up value of credit period vs value of settlement discounts
- Negotiate better terms for large quantities
- Reconcile suppliers' statements carefully
- Pay only once delivery is complete
- Look for improved terms and consider switching

Managing trade receivables

Managing trade receivables

TRADE-OFFS RE GRANTING CREDIT TO CUSTOMERS

COSTS	vs	BENEFITS
■ **Financing costs**		■ Increased sales
■ **Irrecoverable debts**		■ Larger profits
■ Administration		

- Shorten cash cycle
- Avoid bad debts

Grant credit to customers?

Credit rating

Determines whether/how much credit should be extended to a customer.

Consider
■ Ability of customer to pay
■ Analysis of financial statements
■ Using credit rating
■ Trading experience with customer
■ Credit limits
■ References

Credit terms and settlement discounts

Influenced by trade custom

■ **Credit period** eg. 30 days credit
■ **Settlement discount** eg. 2% discount for payment within 10 days

Collection procedures

Should ensure customers pay within credit period

Calculate
■ Cost of discount vs benefit of quicker receipt
■ Effect on cash flows
■ Effect on profit (reduced

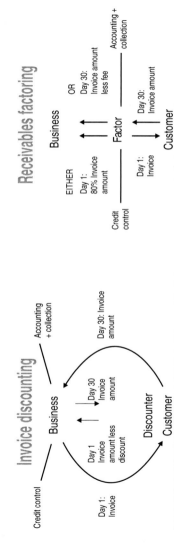

Invoice discounting

Credit control

Day 1: Invoice

Business — Day 1: Invoice amount less discount → **Discounter** → **Customer**

Day 30 Invoice amount

Day 30: Invoice amount

Accounting + collection

Receivables factoring

Credit control

Business

EITHER Day 1: 80% Invoice amount

OR Day 30: Invoice amount less fee

Accounting + collection

Factor

Day 1: Invoice

Day 30: Invoice amount

Customer

Managing receivables well

- Key accounts: 20:80 rule
- Reduce order → sale time
- Invoice immediately/send credit notes promptly
- Reduce invoice → collection time: monitor receivables ageing

- Personal contract
- Link sales commission to cash received, not invoices
- Set targets
- Take out credit insurance

7: Working capital

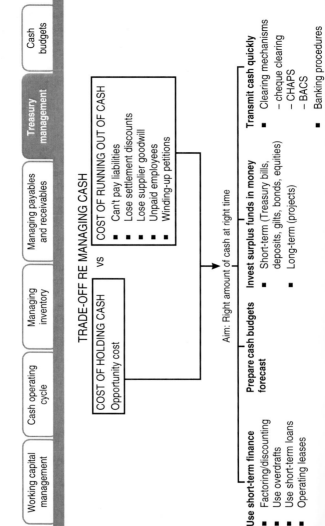

Working capital management | **Cash operating cycle** | **Managing inventory** | **Managing payables and receivables** | **Treasury management** | **Cash budgets**

TRADE-OFF RE MANAGING CASH

COST OF HOLDING CASH	vs	COST OF RUNNING OUT OF CASH
Opportunity cost		▪ Can't pay liabilities
		▪ Lose settlement discounts
		▪ Lose supplier goodwill
		▪ Unpaid employees
		▪ Winding-up petitions

Aim: Right amount of cash at right time

Use short-term finance
- Factoring/discounting
- Use overdrafts
- Use short-term loans
- Operating leases

Prepare cash budgets forecast

Invest surplus funds in money
- Short-term (Treasury bills, deposits, gilts, bonds, equities)
- Long-term (projects)

Transmit cash quickly
- Clearing mechanisms
  - cheque clearing
  - CHAPS
  - BACS
- Banking procedures

Capital markets

- **London Stock Exchange:**

  ① **Main market,** with firm regulation, for raising funds through new issues of shares (primary market), and trading existing shares (secondary market).

  ② **Alternative Investment Market:** for newer companies, less firmly regulated.

- **Gilt edged market** for UK government stock.

- **International capital markets** are operated between banks in larger countries to provide major finance for very large companies and institutions. Confusingly, their securities are known as eurobonds.

- Certain stocks not traded on recognised stock exchanges are traded in **over the counter** markets.

Money markets

Short-term investment and borrowing of funds is handled in the **money markets.** These are operated by the banks and other financial institutions and include markets for:

- Certificates of deposit
- Bills of exchange and commercial paper
- Treasury bills
- Building society bulk borrowing
- Local authority bills and other short-term borrowing

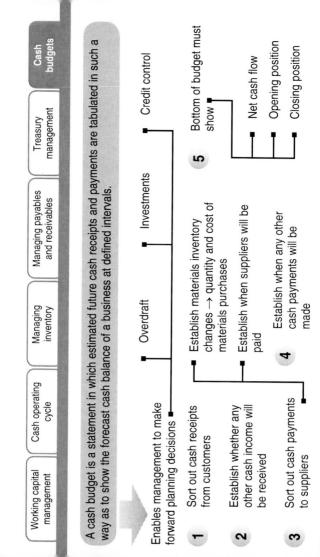

| Working capital management | Cash operating cycle | Managing inventory | Managing payables and receivables | Treasury management | Cash budgets |

A cash budget is a statement in which estimated future cash receipts and payments are tabulated in such a way as to show the forecast cash balance of a business at defined intervals.

Enables management to make forward planning decisions

1 Sort out cash receipts from customers

2 Establish whether any other cash income will be received

3 Sort out cash payments to suppliers

Overdraft

Investments

Credit control

4
- Establish materials inventory changes → quantity and cost of materials purchases
- Establish when suppliers will be paid
- Establish when any other cash payments will be made

5 Bottom of budget must show
- Net cash flow
- Opening position
- Closing position

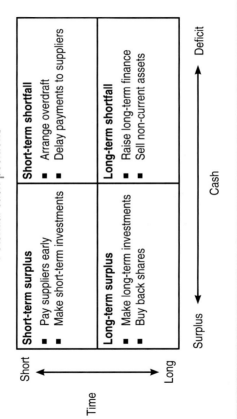

Potential cash positions

Short	**Short-term surplus**	**Short-term shortfall**
	■ Pay suppliers early	■ Arrange overdraft
	■ Make short-term investments	■ Delay payments to suppliers
	Long-term surplus	**Long-term shortfall**
Long	■ Make long-term investments	■ Raise long-term finance
	■ Buy back shares	■ Sell non-current assets

Time

Surplus ←————— Cash —————→ Deficit

PROFORMA CASH BUDGET

	Month 1 £	Month 2 £	Month 3 £
Cash receipts			
Receipts from customers	X	X	X
Loans etc	X	X	X
	X	X	X
Cash payments			
Payments to suppliers	X	X	X
Wages etc	X	X	X
	X	X	X
Net cash flow (receipts – payments)	X	X	X
Opening balance	X	X	X
Closing balance	X	X	X

8: Performance management

Organisations need to monitor how well each part is working toward the achievement of overall objectives.

Performance management systems enable the overall organisation and individual managers to track achievement against targets set.

Cloud accounting is a relatively new system of providing management information. Being able to access real time information from anywhere is a huge benefit.

Topic List

Performance evaluation

Responsibility centres

Cloud accounting

Performance measures

Balanced scorecard

Budgetary control

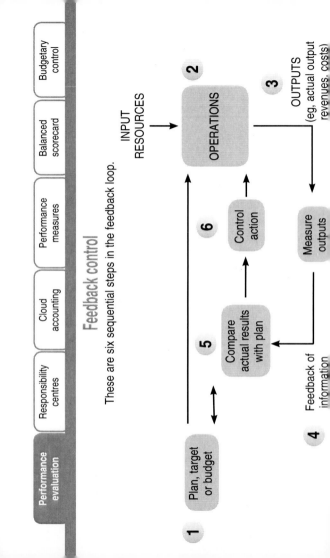

Feedback control

These are six sequential steps in the feedback loop.

Performance evaluation | Responsibility centres | Cloud accounting | Performance measures | Balanced scorecard | Budgetary control

1. Plan, target or budget
2. OPERATIONS
3. OUTPUTS (eg, actual output revenues, costs)
4. Feedback of information
5. Compare actual results with plan
6. Control action

INPUT RESOURCES

Measure outputs

Budget style and management performance

BUDGET	STYLE OF EVALUATION
Important	→ Budget constrained
Budget used to assess performance	→ Profit conscious
Unimportant	→ Non-accounting

Effective feedback

- Clear and comprehensive
- Exception principle applies
- Controllable costs and revenues identified clearly
- Regular reporting
- Timely reporting
- Accurate information
- Audience is responsible manager

Divisionalisation

Involves splitting the organisation into divisions, eg, according to location or product.

In general, a divisional structure will lead to decentralisation of the decision-making process.

Advantages of decentralisation

- ☑ It can improve the decision-making process in two ways.
  - Quality
  - Speed
- ☑ The authority to act to improve performance should motivate divisional managers.
- ☑ Top management are freed from detailed involvement in day-to-day operations and can devote more time to strategic planning.
- ☑ Divisions provide valuable training grounds for future members of top management.

Advantages of decentralisation

- ☒ **Dysfunctional decision making** (a balance has to be kept between decentralisation of authority to provide incentives and motivation, and retaining centralised authority to ensure **goal congruence**)
- ☒ Increase in costs of activities common to all divisions
- ☒ Loss of control by top management

Responsibility accounting

is a system that segregates revenue and costs into areas of personal responsibility.

Cost centre

acts as a collecting place for certain costs before they are analysed further.

Cost centres may include the following:

- A department
- A machine or group of machines
- A project (eg, the installation of a new computer system)
- A new product (allowing developing costs to be identified)

Responsibility centre

is a unit headed by a manager with direct responsibility for its performance.

Profit centre

is any unit or division of a company to which both revenues and costs are assigned, so that the profitability of the unit may be measured.

Profit centres **account for both costs and revenues**. Their **key performance measure** is profit.

The manager of the profit centre normally has some influence over both revenues and costs.

| Performance evaluation | Responsibility centres | Cloud accounting | Performance measures | Balanced scorecard | Budgetary control |

Revenue centre

is accountable for revenues only.

For revenue centres to have any validity, a planning and control system is based on revenue responsibility. Revenue centre managers should normally have control over how revenues are raised.

Investment centre

is a profit centre whose performance is measured by its return on capital employed.

The investment centre manager has some say in investment policy in his or her area of operations, as well as being responsible for costs and revenues.

Shared service centres

Shared service centres consolidate the transaction-processing activities of many operations within a company. Functions such as human resources, payroll, accounting and IT may be carried out in a shared service centre.

Advantages to using a shared service centre include:

- Reduced headcount due to economies of scale
- Associated reduction in premises and other overhead costs
- Knowledge sharing should lead to an improvement in quality of the service provided
- Allows standard approaches to be adopted across the organisation leading to more consistent management of business data

Disadvantages include:

- Loss of business specific knowledge.
- Removed from decision making.
- Weakened relationships (particularly due to geographical distance).
- Cost inefficiencies could be passed on to the client division leading to friction.

Performance evaluation	Responsibility centres	**Cloud accounting**	Performance measures	Balanced scorecard	Budgetary control

Cloud computing

'Is a model for enabling ubiquitous, convenient, on-demand network access to a shared pool of configurable computing resources (eg, networks, servers, storage, applications and services) that can be 'rapidly provisioned and released with minimal management effort or service provider interaction'. (US Department of Commerce, National Institute of Standards and Technology)

Cloud accounting

An application of cloud computing where accountancy software is provided in the cloud by a service provider.

Benefits of cloud accounting

- Accounting information can be accessed from anywhere, at any time, using the internet.
- Security systems will often be better than a small business can provide.
- Software updates are managed by the cloud accounting supplier.
- Back ups are made automatically by the cloud accounting supplier.
- Applications are usually rented rather than purchased ie, no upfront costs.
- Overhead costs, such as in-house technical experts costs, can be reduced.
- No need for powerful PCs as the software is running in the cloud.
- Collaboration between users is easier as files can be shared via invitations.
- If the business grows then more cloud accounting licences can be purchased.

Risks of cloud accounting

- The supplier could fail and so a contingency plan is required.
- There is a permanent need for internet access.
- There is a risk of security breaches, including data loss or theft and privacy issues.
- There are legislation risks if the cloud supplier operates from a jurisdiction where the laws are different from the country in which the data is being used (particularly privacy laws).
- Unannounced changes or upgrades to software could be disruptive.

Performance measurement is a vital part of control and aims to establish how well something or somebody is doing in relation to a planned activity.

Performance measures

Effective

- ☑ Promote goal congruence
- ☑ Measure controllable factors only
- ☑ Encourage long-term objectives

Ineffective

- ☒ Manipulate information
- ☒ Cause demotivation
- ☒ Over emphasise short-term objectives
- ☒ Isolated measures

Cost centre

- Cost variances
- Cost per unit
- Cost per employee
- Labour turnover

Revenue centre

- Revenue variances
- Revenue per employee
- Market share
- Revenue growth

Profit centre

- Gross profit margin
- Operating profit margin

Investment centre

- Liquidity means (eg, quick ratio)
- Rare of inventory turnover
- Receivables and payables periods
- ROI
- RI

| Performance evaluation | Responsibility centres | Cloud accounting | Performance measures | Balanced scorecard | Budgetary control |

Investment centres

ROI

Calculated as (controllable divisional profit/capital employed) x 100%, using pre-tax profit and average of opening and closing capital.

- Measures **efficiency** with which capital employed (**input**) used to generate profit (**value of output**)
- Increased by improving profit margins and/or increasing asset turnover

RI

Calculated as divisional profit less notional interest.

- Avoids the manipulation of capital employed with the use of ROI

RI versus ROI

☑ More flexible than ROI

☑ RI improves when investments earn above hurdle rate

☒ ROI can be open to manipulation of capital employed eg, age of assets, depreciation policy

☒ RI can't be used for comparisons between investment centres

☒ RI doesn't relate size of income to investment

Perspective	Detail	Examples
Financial	Concerned with satisfying shareholders	■ ROCE ■ Sales margin
Customer	Attempts to measure how customers view the organisation and how they measure customer satisfaction	■ Delivery speed, measured by time between order and delivery ((orders received in yr − net sales/net sales) × 365 days) ■ Customer loyalty, measured by repeat business ((turnover from regular customers/total turnover) × 100%)
Internal business efficiency	Measures the quality of the organisation's outputs in terms of technical excellence and consumer needs	■ Total quality measurement (reworked faulty production as % of total production) ■ Training costs as a % of production costs ■ Resource utilisation measures (eg, proportion of available hotel rooms occupied)
Innovation and learning	Emphasises the need for continual improvement of existing products and the ability to develop new products to meet customers' changing needs	■ Turnover from new products as % of total turnover

Fixed budgets

These are budgets which are set for a single activity level. Master budgets are fixed budgets.

vs

Flexible budgets

These are budgets which, by recognising different cost behaviours patterns, change as activity levels change.

To **prepare a flexible budget**:

1. Decide whether costs are fixed, variable or semi-variable, and split semi-variable costs using the high/low method

2. Calculate the budget cost allowance for each item = budgeted fixed cost* + (number of units × variable cost per unit)**

* nil for variable cost   ** nil for fixed cost

Using flexible budgets for control

1. Produce a flexible budget based on the **actual** activity level.

2. Compare the flexible budget with the fixed budget, and with actual results.

3. Identify variances.

   Volume variance = difference between fixed budget and flexible budget

   Expenditure variance = difference between flexible budget and actual results

9: Standard costing and variance analysis

In a standard costing system, standard costs are devised for each cost unit for **price** and **quantity** of resources used.

This allows comparisons to be made with actual results and variances are calculated.

These variances can be interpreted and action taken as needed.

Topic List

Standard costs and costing

Cost variances

Sales variances and operating statements

Interpreting variances and actual costs

Standard costing

is a control technique that reports variances by comparing actual costs to pre-set standards so facilitating action through management by exception.

Uses

- To value inventories and cost production
- To act as a control device via variance analysis

Standard costs

The total standard cost of a product is built up from standards for each cost element. These must be monitored to ensure that they are reasonable and reliable.

Advantages

- ☑ Aid accurate budgeting
- ☑ Yard stick for measuring actual costs
- ☑ Promote **cost consciousness**
- ☑ Simplify bookkeeping
- ☑ Provide incentives for employees

STANDARD COST CARD
PRODUCT LW

	£
Direct material (standard quantity × standard price)	X
Direct labour (standard time × standard rate)	X
Standard direct cost	X
Variable production overhead (standard time × standard rate)	X
Standard variable cost of production	X
Fixed production overhead (standard time × standard rate)	X
Standard full production cost	X
Administration and marketing overhead	X
Standard cost of sale	X
Standard profit	X
Standard selling price	X

Example

Product LW has a standard direct material cost as follows.

10 kg of material M at £10 per kg = £100 per unit of M.

During a period, 1,000 units of LW were manufactured, using 11,700 kg of material M, which cost £98,600.

Direct material total variance

	£
1,000 units should have cost	100,000
but did cost	98,600
Direct material total variance	1,400 (F)

Direct material price

	£
11,700 kg of M should have cost	117,000
but did cost	98,600
Material M price variance	18,400 (F)

Direct material usage

1,000 units should have used (× 10 kg)	10,000 kg
but did use	11,700 kg
Usage variance in kgs	1,700 kg (A)
× standard cost per kilogram	× £10
Material M usage variance	£17,000 (A)

Direct material cost variance = material price variance + material usage variance

Example

The standard direct labour cost of product LW is as follows.

2 hours of grade A labour at £5 per hour = £10 per unit of product LW

During a period, 1,500 units of product LW were made, and the direct labour cost of grade A labour was £17,500 for 3,080 hours of work.

Direct labour total variance

	£
1,500 units of product LW should have cost (× £10)	15,000
but did cost	17,500
Direct labour total variance	2,500 (A)

Direct labour rate variance

	£
3,080 hours of grade A labour should have cost (× £5)	15,400
but did cost	17,500
Direct labour rate variance	2,100 (A)

Direct labour efficiency variance

1,500 units of product LW should take (× 2 hours)	3,000 hrs
but did take (3,080)	3,080 hrs
Direct labour efficiency variance in hrs	80 hrs (A)
× standard rate per hour	× £5
Direct labour efficiency variance in £	400 (A)

Direct labour total variance = labour rate variance + labour efficiency variance

9: Standard costing and variance analysis

Variable production overhead variances

Variable overhead total variance

	£
400 units	
should cost (× £3)	1,230
but did cost	1,360
Total variance	160 (A)

Expenditure variance

	£
820 hours of var. prod. o'head	
should cost (× £1.50)	1,230
but did cost	1,360
Variable production overhead expenditure variance	130 (A)

Example

The variable production overhead cost of product LW is as follows.

2 hours @ £1.50 = £3 per unit

During a period, 400 units of product LW were made. The labour force worked 820 hours. The variable overhead cost was £1,360.

Efficiency variance

400 units of product LW should take (× 2 hrs) but did take (active)	800 hrs
	820 hrs
Variable prod. o'head efficiency variance in hours	20 hrs (A)
× standard rate per hour	× £1.50
Variable production overhead efficiency variance in £	£30 (A)

Fixed overhead expenditure variance

is simply the difference between the budgeting and actual fixed overhead expenditure in the period.

= Budgeting fixed overhead cost – Actual fixed overhead cost

Selling price variance

is a measure of the effect on expected revenue of a different selling price to standard selling price.

Sales volume variance

is the difference between actual units sold and the budgeted quantity, valued at the standard contribution per unit.

Example

The standard selling price of product H is £15. Actual sales in 2001 were 2,000 units at £15.30 per unit. Budgeted sales were 2,200 units and standard variable cost per unit of H is £12.30.

Selling price variance

	£
Sales revenue from 2,000 units should have been (× £15)	30,000
but was (× £15.30)	30,600
Selling price variance	600 (F)

Favourable variance because the price was higher than expected

Sales volume variance

Budgeted sales volume	2,200
Actual sales volume	2,000
	200 (A)
× standard contribution per unit (£15 − £12.30)	× £2.70
Sales volume variance	540 (A)

Adverse variance because actual sales volume was less than budgeted

An operating statement is a regular report for management of actual cost and revenues, as appropriate. It will usually compare actual with budget to show variances.

OPERATING STATEMENT

	Favourable	Adverse	
			£
Budgeted contribution			X
Sales volume variance			X
Sales price variance			X
Actual sales less standard variable cost of sales			X
	Favourable	**Adverse**	
VARIABLE COST VARIANCES	£	£	£
Material price	X		
Material usage etc		X	
Total variable cost variances	X	X	X
ACTUAL CONTRIBUTION			X
		£	
Budgeted fixed overhead		X	
Fixed overhead expenditure variance		X	
Actual fixed overhead		X	X
Actual profit			X

> Operating statements sometimes reconcile budgeted profit to actual profit.

OPERATING STATEMENT

	Favourable	Adverse	Interpreting variances and actual costs
	£	£	£
Budgeted profit			X
Sales volume variance		X	
Sales price variance	X		
COST VARIANCES			
Materials price	X		
Materials usage		X	
Labour rate		X	
Labour efficiency		X	
Variable overhead rate		X	
Variable overhead efficiency		X	
Fixed overhead expenditure		X	
TOTAL VARIANCES	X	X	
Actual profit			X

Material price

Favourable
Unforeseen discounts
Material std changed

Adverse
Price increase
Careless purchasing

Variable and fixed overhead

Favourable
Cost savings

Adverse
Excessive use

Sales price

Favourable
Original selling price
too low

Adverse
Original selling price
too high

Material usage

Favourable
Higher quality material
Effective use of material

Adverse
Defective material
Excessive waste

Labour rate

Favourable
Lower rate paid

Adverse
Wage rate increase

Labour efficiency

Favourable
Motivated staff

Adverse
Lack of training

Sales volume

Favourable
Efficient sales force

Adverse
Demotivated sales force

9: Standard costing and variance analysis

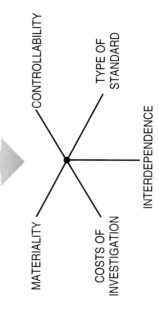

Significant variances should be investigated. Factors to take into account:

- CONTROLLABILITY
- TYPE OF STANDARD
- INTERDEPENDENCE
- COSTS OF INVESTIGATION
- MATERIALITY

Interdependence

The cause of one variance (adverse) might be wholly or partly explained by the cause of another favourable variance.

- Material price and usage variances
- Material price and labour efficiency variances
- Labour rate and efficiency variances
- Sales price and sales volume
- Cost and sales variance

10: Breakeven analysis and limiting factor analysis

Managers need to be aware of how costs change when decisions are made. They can then work out measures such as the activity required to break even.

Understanding the contribution earned by products and services will also help managers to allocate scarce resources to maximise contribution.

Topic List

Breakeven analysis and contribution

Breakeven charts

Limiting factor analysis

Breakeven analysis and contribution | Breakeven charts | Limiting factor analysis

Contribution per unit

is unit selling price – unit variable costs.

Contribution ratio

is a measure of how much contribution is earned from each £1 of sales revenue.

Breakeven point

is activity level at which there is neither profit nor loss.

$$\frac{\text{Total fixed costs}}{\text{Contribution per unit}} \longleftrightarrow \boxed{\text{Breakeven point}} \longleftrightarrow \frac{\text{Contribution required to break even}}{\text{Contribution ratio}}$$

Breakeven point → Sales revenue at breakeven point

The margin of safety is the difference in units between the budgeted sales volume and the breakeven sales volume and it is sometimes expressed as a percentage of the budgeted sales volume.

The sales volume to achieve a target profit = $\dfrac{\text{Fixed costs + target profit}}{\text{Contribution per unit}}$

> ### Example
>
> Selling price = £15 per unit
> Variable cost = £12 per unit
> Fixed costs = £5,400 per annum
> Budgeted sales pa = 3,000 units

- Breakeven point (units) = $\dfrac{£5,400}{£15 - £12}$ = 1,800 units

- Contribution ratio = 3/15 × 100% = 20% = 0.2

- Breakeven point (revenue) = $\dfrac{5,400}{0.2}$ = £27,000

- Sales volume to achieve profit of £3,300 = $\dfrac{£(5,400 + 3,300)}{£3}$ = 2,900 units

- Margin of safety (as a %) = $\dfrac{3,000 - 1,800}{3,000}$ × 100% = 40%

10: Breakeven analysis and limiting factor analysis

Breakeven chart

Shows the approximate level of profit or loss at different sales volume levels within a limited range.

- Profit/loss is the difference between the sales revenue line and the total costs line

- The breakeven point is where the total costs line and the sales revenue line meet

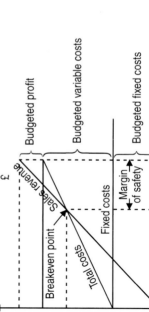

Contribution breakeven chart

Draw the variable costs line instead of the fixed costs line.

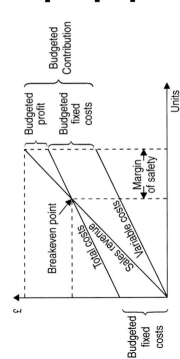

- This type of chart shows clearly the contribution for different levels of production

- At the breakeven point, contribution = fixed costs

- Contribution = Sales revenue line – variable costs line

10: Breakeven analysis and limiting factor analysis

Limiting factor situations

Scenario	How to maximise contribution/profit	Detail
Sales demand restricts production/output	Make exactly the amount required for sales (and no more) provided that each product sold earns a positive contribution	
One scarce resource (such as material or labour)	Earn the biggest possible contribution per unit of scarce resource	Assume fixed costs remain unchanged whatever the production mix, the only relevant costs being variable costs
One limiting factor and restrictions on sales demand or two potentially limiting factors	Rank products in order of contribution-earning ability per unit of limiting factor but produce the top-ranked products up to the sales demand limit	Although there may appear to be more than one scarce resource, it may be that there is no limiting factor except sales demand or that there is only one scarce resource that prevents full potential sales demand being achieved

Profit will be maximised when contribution is maximised.

The profit-maximising product mix might not be possible because the mix is also restricted by a factor other than a scarce resource.

In such circumstances the organisation might have to produce more of a particular product or products than the level established by ranking according to contribution per unit of limiting factor.

Factors that restrict freedom of action

- A contract to supply a certain number of products
- Provision of a complete product range and/or maintenance of customer goodwill
- Maintenance of a certain market share

Basic approach

1 Confirm that the limiting factor is not sales demand.

2 Rank the products in the normal way.

3 Take account of the minimum production requirements within the optimum production plan.

4 Allocate the remaining resources according to the ranking.

10: Breakeven analysis and limiting factor analysis

Make or buy decisions and scarce resources

Suppose a company must subcontract work to make up a shortfall in its own production capacity.

Its total costs are minimised if those units bought have the lowest extra variable cost of buying per unit of scarce resource saved.

Example

A company, which makes three products, has limited labour time available.

	A £	B £	C £
Variable cost of making	10	16	14
Variable cost of buying	19	20	19
Extra variable cost of buying	9	4	5
Labour hours saved by buying (per unit)	3	2	2
Extra variable cost of buying per hour saved	£3	£2	£2.50
Priority for making in-house	1st	3rd	2nd

11: Investment appraisal techniques

Capital expenditure differs from revenue expenditure. Thus:

- *It involves a larger outlay of cash*
- *Benefits accrue over a long period of time*

There are several techniques that are available to make capital spending decisions. These range in their usefulness. Make sure you know where each technique is most suitable to use.

Topic List

Investment appraisal decisions

Payback

Accounting rate of return

Net present value (NPV)

Internal rate of return (IRR)

NPV vs IRR

Investment appraisal decisions	Payback	Accounting rate of return	Net present value (NPV)	Internal rate of return (IRR)	NPV vs IRR

Investment decision-making process

1 Origination of proposals

Set up a mechanism which scans the environment for potential opportunities and provides an early warning of future problems.

2 Project screening

Carry out a qualitative evaluation:

- Purpose
- 'Fit' with long-term objectives
- Alternatives

3 Analysis and acceptance

- Submit standard format financial information as a formal investment proposal
- Consider qualitative and quantitative issues
- Carry out financial analysis

4 Monitoring and review

- Control over excess spending
- Control over delays
- Control over anticipated benefits

Payback

The time it takes the cash inflows (**≈ profits before depreciation**) from an investment to equal the cash outflows, usually expressed in years.

It is often used as a first screening method, the project being evaluated with a more sophisticated technique if it gets through the payback test.

Decision rules

1 When deciding between two or more competing projects, the usual decision is to accept the one with the shortest payback.

2 Reject a project if its payback is greater than a target payback.

11: Investment appraisal techniques

Disadvantages

☒ It ignores the timing of cash flows within the payback period, the cash flows after the end of the payback period and hence the total project return.

☒ It ignores the time value of money.

☒ It makes no distinction between different projects with the same payback period.

☒ The choice of cut-off payback period is arbitrary.

☒ The method may lead to excessive investment in short-term projects.

☒ It takes account of the risk associated with the timing of cash flows but not the variability of those cash flows.

Advantages

☑ Long payback means capital is tied up.

☑ A focus on early payback can enhance liquidity.

☑ Investment risk is increased if payback is longer.

☑ Shorter-term forecasts are likely to be more reliable.

☑ The calculation is quick and simple.

☑ Payback is an easily understood concept.

Accounting rate of return (ARR)

There are several definitions of ARR (the method selected should be used consistently) but the two recommended definitions are

$$ARR = \frac{\text{Average annual accounting profit}}{\text{Average investment}} \times 100\%$$

$$ARR = \frac{\text{Average annual accounting profit}}{\text{Initial investment}} \times 100\%$$

- **Annual profits are after depreciation**
- Average investment = ½(initial cost + residual value)

If you are not provided with a figure for profit, assume that net cash inflow minus depreciation equals profit.

Decision rules

- **One project**
  - If the ARR is greater than the target rate of return, accept the project.
  - If the ARR is less than the target rate of return, reject the project.

- **When comparing two or more mutually exclusive projects, the project with the highest ARR should be chosen (provided the ARR is greater than the target ARR).**

Advantages

☑ Quick and simple

☑ Looks at the entire project life

☑ Easily calculated from financial statements

☑ An appraisal method that employs profit may be more easily understood

Disadvantages

☒ Takes no account of the timing of cash flows

☒ Based on accounting profits which are subject to a number of different accounting treatments

☒ Takes no account of the size of the investment or the length of the project

☒ Ignores the time value of money

Example

Equipment J has a capital cost of £100,000 and a disposal value of £20,000 at the end of its five-year life. Profits before depreciation over the five years total £150,000.

∴ Total profit after depreciation = £(150,000 – 80,000) = £70,000

Average annual profit after depreciation = £14,000

(Capital cost + disposal cost) / 2 = £60,000

ARR = (14/60) × 100% = 20%

Present value

The cash equivalent now (X) of a sum of money (V) receivable or payable at the end of n time periods.

Discounting provides the formula $X = V/(1+r)^n$, where r is the rate of return.

Compounding provides the formula $V = X(1+r)^n$ which is the **terminal value** of an investment.

Net present value

The value obtained by discounting all cash inflows and outflows of a capital investment project by a chosen target rate of return.

Organisations may use different discount rates over the life of a project to reflect interest and inflation.

Decision rules

- **When comparing two or more mutually exclusive projects, the project with the highest positive NPV should be selected.**

- **One project**
  - If NPV > 0 ▶ accept project
  - If NPV < 0 ▶ reject project

11: Investment appraisal techniques

Time value of money

Why is £1 now more than £1 in the future?

- Uncertainty
- Inflation
- More weight is attached to current pleasures than to those occurring in the future

Discount factors

Present value tables cover integer costs of capital from 1% to 20% for 1 to 20 years. If you require a discount factor for a non-integer interest rate (say 12.5%) or a period of time greater than 20 years, use $1/(1+r)^n$, where r = cost of capital and n = number of years

Timing of cash flows

- A cash outlay to be incurred at the beginning of an investment project ('**now**') occurs at time 0 and will have a present value = outlay (since PV of £1 now = £1)
- A cash flow occurring **during the course of a time period** is assumed to occur at the end of the time period
- A cash flow occurring **at the beginning of a time period** is assumed to occur at the end of the previous time period

Perpetuities

An annual cash flow in perpetuity. (An annuity that lasts forever.)

The PV of £1 pa in perpetuity at r% = £1/r (where r is a decimal).

Net terminal value (NTV)

The cash surplus remaining at the end of a project after taking account of interest and capital repayments.

The NTV discounted at the cost of capital = NPV

Other aspects of discounting

1 Delayed annuities   **2** Annuities in advance

Annuities

A constant annual cash flow from year to year.

Use discount factors from **cumulative present value tables.**

Discounted payback

combines **payback** with **DCF** to calculate a **discounted payback period (DPP)**.

The DPP is the time it will take before a project's cumulative NPV turns from being negative to being positive.

IRR

The rate of interest at which the NPV of an investment is zero.

Decision rule

If the IRR is greater than the target rate of return, the project is worth undertaking.

IRR of a perpetuity

- IRR = perpetuity ÷ initial investment

Graphical approach

Suppose a project has the following NPVs at the following discount rates.

Discount rate	NPV
%	£
5	5,300
10	2,900
15	(1,700)
20	(3,200)

These can be easily plotted on a graph.

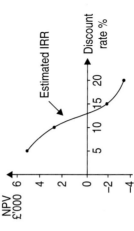

Recalculate the NPV using the estimated IRR (from the graph) of 13% and if the resulting NPV is not equal to, or very near, zero, additional NPVs at different discount rates should be calculated, the graph redrawn and a more accurate IRR determined.

11: Investment appraisal techniques

Interpolation method

1. Calculate the NPV using a rough indicator of the IRR ($^2/_3$ (or $^3/_4$) × ARR).

   Remember you will need to account for depreciation and any residual value when determining the ARR.

2. If the resulting NPV > 0, recalculate the NPV using a higher rate.

3. If the resulting NPV < 0, recalculate the NPV using a lower rate.

   The closer these NPVs are to zero, the closer the estimate to the true IRR.

4. $IRR = a + \dfrac{NPVa}{NPVa - NPVb} \ (b - a)$

   where a is the first discount rate giving NPVa
          b is the second discount rate giving NPVb

NPV vs IRR

Which is better?

	NPV	IRR
When cash flow patterns are conventional both methods give the same accept or reject decision	☑	☑
The IRR method is more easily understood		☑
IRR and ROCE/ROI can be confused	☑	
IRR ignores the relative sizes of investments	☑	
When cash flow patterns are non-conventional there may be several IRRs of which decision makers must be aware to avoid making the wrong decision	☑	
The NPV method is superior for ranking mutually exclusive projects in order of attractiveness	☑	
When discount rates are expected to differ over the life of the project, such variations can be incorporated easily into NPV calculations but not into IRR calculations	☑	

Despite the advantages of the NPV method over the IRR method, the IRR method is widely used in practice.

11: Investment appraisal techniques

Notes

Notes